Poems from the Heart

Poems from the Heart

Jenny Jones

ATHENA PRESS
LONDON

POEMS FROM THE HEART

ISBN 978 1 84748 267 9

First published 2008 by
ATHENA PRESS
Queen's House, 2 Holly Road
Twickenham TW1 4EG
United Kingdom

Printed for Athena Press

This book is dedicated to my father, Trevor William Jones,
who passed away on 28 January 2007

Introduction

These poems contain my thoughts and experiences over the past twenty years. I started writing songs first, then made them into poems. The poems are quite varied and people who have read them all have their own favourites. I really hope you like them. Over the past couple of years several friends have encouraged me to publish my poems, so I thought, as they liked them so much, I would give it a go! The more emotional poems are inspired by my own relationships. The others poems are based on my feelings and thoughts about the world.

Contents

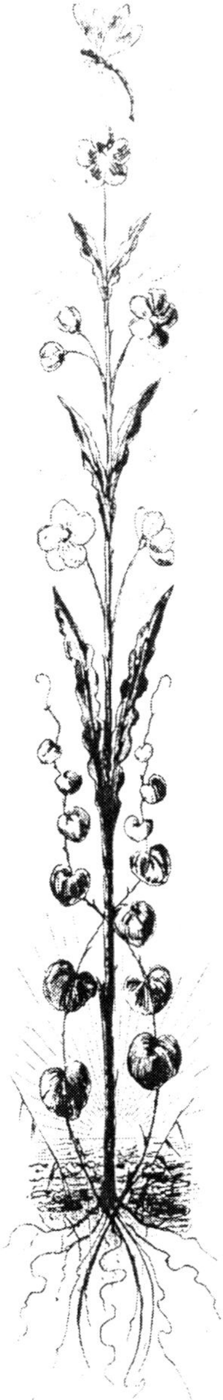

Father of the Year

Father of the year, it's got to be,
Because you've been so good to me.
You're the greatest father in the world,
I won't ever forget what you've done for
me.

You're an extra-special parent,
Whom I admire so very much;
You know I hold a lot of respect for you,
Without making too much of a fuss.

I'll always care and love you,
Through the rough times and the good,
You'll always be my number one,
Which will always be for good.

Dedicated to my Dad

I'll miss you very much, Dad;
I know you'll be watching over me
As I carry on with my life.
You'll never be forgotten, now you're free;
You'll always be with me, for ever and a day;
In my heart and mind you'll always stay.

I'll never forget how you looked after me;
I won't forget what you taught me, too.
I'll remember you for your sense of humour,
And how you made me laugh through and
through.

You were the sort of person
Who'd do anything for anyone.
Without expecting anything in return
You were always kind and loveable;
So I'll never forget all that
I ever learned from you.

Summer Falls

The leaves are so green in the summer,
The sun starts shining through,
The flowers they all keep growing,
Just for the likes of me and you.

The trees they sway so freely,
Just like they are intended to do,
The birds they sing so sweetly,
Just like god wanted them to.

All the clouds are black and grey,
Holding rain as they should do,
So the world does not dry up,
They let the rain break through.

I love to walk along the lake,
And see the sun shine on it;
It's such a lovely sight to see,
It makes the world so sweet to me.

Lonely Teenager

I was alone as a teenage girl,
Then I found the man of my dreams.
Morning by morning, I would see him,
And I'd fall apart at the seams.

Day by day I would see him,
I'd dream to be by his side,
But I knew I was only dreaming –
He'd got someone else by his side.

So I'm left with sorrow in my heart,
Tears that won't go away;
I know that I will never catch him,
So I'll leave and be on my way.

Shall I Ever Find Love?

What is love? I really don't know,
I haven't really found it yet;
So I'm having my doubts, you know,
What is love? Does it really exist?
If it does I'm sure I'll find it,
And I'm sure he'll be a whiz.

People try and tell me, 'You'll find the one,
You might have to wait a while,
But I'm sure you'll have your fun.'
Waiting is a frustrating game,
But it'll be worth it in the end,
Coz when you find the one you love,
He'll treat you right, up until the end.

It's a question I ask every day as I live,
Though I know I shouldn't worry,
Yet something has to give –
What is life if you're living on your own?
You need to share your feelings,
So you don't ever feel alone.

The Two of Us

Meeting the man of your dreams
Is harder than it seems,
When you find one who cares for you,
It's never as straight as it seems:
He'll say he cares and loves you
But knowing all along
You're not the one he really loves –
He'll soon be moving on.

Walking along the narrow lane,
Asking myself who is to blame,
Knowing it's going to take a while
To shake off all this pain.
Thinking to myself how it used to be,
Wondering what went wrong,
Trying to find some answers,
While I'm listening to my songs.

Jealousy is a dangerous thing,
It ruins lives every day –
Feeling very insecure,
Worrying what others might say.
When you find the one for you,
You'll feel it straight away.
That's when you feel happy and complete,
In each and every way.

Waiting at the Airport

While we are standing at the airport,
Waiting at these gates,
I know I'm going to miss you –
For a while at least, let's say.

Trying to hide our tears,
As I'm waiting to catch my plane,
We both know how the other is feeling,
But nobody is to blame.

We hug each other so tightly,
As they call out my flight's name,
I'm sure to feel a bit afraid,
As I climb aboard my plane.

But I know I will survive
If I imagine you by my side,
Knowing that this is how
I'm going to live my life.

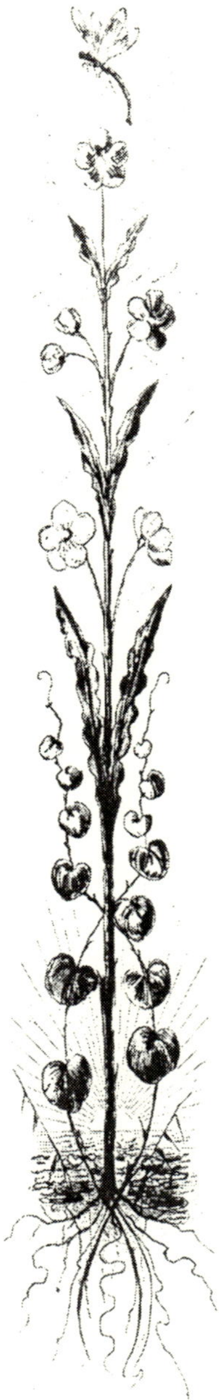

Breaking Up

Meeting someone who will
Cheer you up with a smile;
Knowing you're not attracted to him,
But you really admire his style;
So therefore taking a chance
That it may turn to romance,
Taking that big risk,
That you won't fall into a trance.

I find out more about him:
How he loves the ladies so,
Thinking to myself, Am I
Just another on his road?
Then I find out he has a wife
Whom he hasn't let go –
Stringing other women along
Because of a row at home.

So I make the big decision
That it's better to break up –
Even though I know
That he'll only get the hump.
I'm glad it was only six weeks
Into the relationship,
Coz it didn't take me long
To get over him – only a little bit.

Beautiful Sky

As I look up
At the beautiful sky,
I see a rainbow
That catches my eye.
It's a lovely blue sky,
The sun is so fine;
There are a few raindrops,
But still the sun shines.

We need to take a look
At all the scenery there is;
We need to stop
And take a look around,
Instead of rushing
Every minute of the day –
It'd be nice just to settle and calm down.

The Earth needs to be treasured more;
Stop the trees from being
Chopped for items to store;
Stop the fields being turned over,
When there are already enough houses –
There'll be no grass left
For the little field mouse,
If we don't make a stand;
Think twice about how we act,
Or we'll have nothing left to attract.

Sweet Smile

Your eyes they sparkle
Like the stars in the sky;
Your smile's so sweet
It makes me go wild inside.
You've got me going
Out of my mind;
Why not tell me
How you're feeling inside?

When I see you walking
Down the high street,
I feel so warm,
I'm full of heat.
Your style and look
Make you look so neat –
To look at you
Is a real big treat!

If you take a chance on me,
Ask me out for a cup of tea,
My answer would be yes,
You know it would be,
Coz I've got a crush on you –
Can't you see?

Music is my Life

At the early age of six,
Val Doonican was my hero,
I thought he was bliss
As I sang his songs in the lift.

I'd memorise all the words
To each and every song –
Coz I really loved his music
And loved to sing along.

I would borrow a friend's tape deck,
Which was always in the same place;
I would sit there crossed-legged,
Then sing without any haste…

I was so happy while doing this,
I was so contented,
That nothing else would cross my lips.
I don't know why
I loved those tunes so;
Through my heart and body,
They'd always send a glow.

Life

Life is so precious
And lovely to me,
We should make the most of it –
Do you see?
I hope most people
Would surely agree,
That you should enjoy yourself
And set yourself free.

Treasure the moments
Of each and every day,
Cherish what you've got,
Live in such a way,
To be happy at work –
Work hard and then play.
You only have one chance,
So live fully each day.

We're not here for very long,
We're only here visiting,
We're only here in-between.
So we need to look after the Earth,
Especially the trees,
Also preserve the animals –
I really hope you agree.

Wishing

Since you've gone out of my life for ever,
Each day I feel so sad inside,
Wishing we could be together,
With love and happiness that will thrive.

I know I'm not a woman
Who's got a lot of style,
I know I haven't even
Got a wonderful smile.
But all my love for you
Was honest and true,
You know I would have done
Anything for you.

You always built my hopes up
By saying 'I love you',
I suppose I was the fool
To believe it could've been true.
I always thought you were different
From all those other men,
But I guess that I was wrong –
What more can I say?

I hope we can still be friends
Till the day that I die,
If you're ever on your own,
You don't have to be shy.
I'll always care and love you
So very deep inside,
These feelings of mine
I cannot hide.

Could it be Love?

You know when I first saw you,
I loved you at first sight,
I know I'll never forget you,
I know with all my might.

You'll never know who loves you,
You'll never know who cares,
Unless you open your eyes
To the person who's really there.

I'm not trying to make you love me,
Don't ever think I would,
I know you'll never want me,
I know you never could.

To men it's all a game,
They just don't understand.
One day you'll be so sorry,
And become a real man.

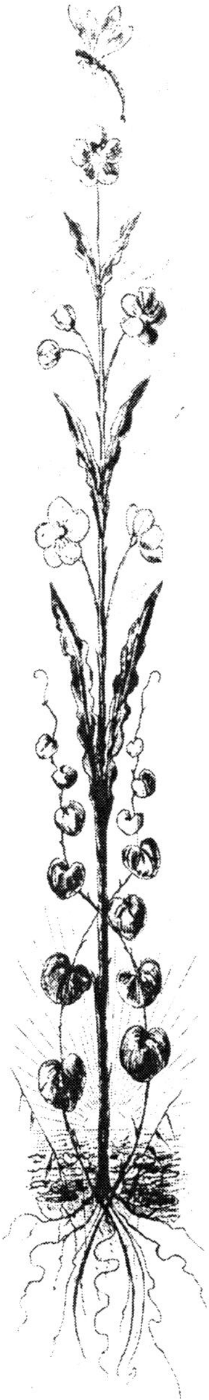

Say You'll Always Love Me

You look and smile so sweetly,
I feel such a warm glow inside,
You make my heart skip a beat,
When you're so near to my side.

You know I'll never forget you,
You'll always be in my mind,
Every time our eyes meet,
I'll always go weak inside.

I know I don't stand a chance,
I'll never be by your side,
Looks and style aren't everything,
What counts is deep down inside.

I'll always care and love you,
You won't know that I exist,
Coz I will never let you know,
I won't show you any hints.

Finding You

You look so great,
I'm glad you're mine,
Shall we go for a stroll?
To pass the time,
Come hold my hand,
And things will be just fine.
So don't be shy,
Let your personality shine.

I really hope you know,
Each day I think of you,
Wondering to myself
Whether you do the same too.
I think, deep in your heart,
You already knew
That my thoughts were only ever
Honestly stuck on you.

So now you know,
Will you dine with me?
I could show you how I feel,
So that you'll be able to see
That there's no need to rush –
Although, it has to be said,
You're everything I'd hoped for
In my heart and in my head.

Fighting Your Illness

You know you're really fit and well in
yourself.
Then, suddenly, you're collapsing to the
ground.
Finding then that you're so unwell,
It leaves you with a frown.

Knowing that you're unable to work,
Finding it very hard to accept,
You then feel down and angry,
Trying not to feel like a reject.

You then pick yourself up off the floor,
Knowing that you'll never give up,
You then start to believe you will be all right,
So you try to stay smiling, not being abrupt.

You then find something worthwhile to do,
Like charity or voluntary work to help others,
You then learn to respect yourself and to
feel useful,
Which puts a smile back on your face,
instead of a shudder.

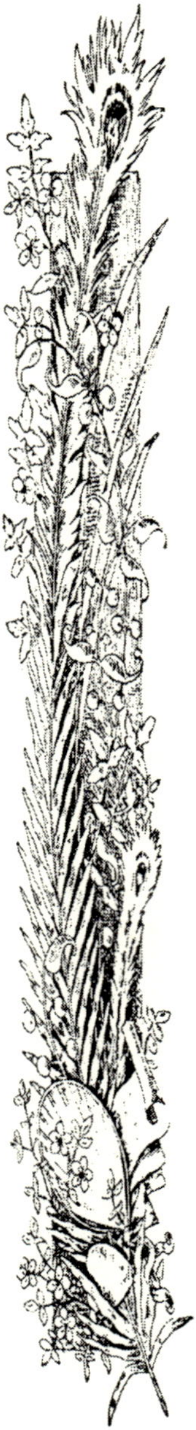

Just Be Yourself

Love is such a special gift,
But we all just throw it away,
Coz we're never careful
In all that we might say.
We need to have been shown,
So we can understand,
Love is such a special gift,
So mind each word you say.

So you wish to choose a partner,
Can I recommend something to you?
You don't need to be so choosy,
Or you'll be left on the shelf too.
If you really do love someone,
You must always let them know,
Coz love doesn't come along every day,
So don't blow it if you know.

You don't need to buy them presents,
Or give them money too,
Coz if you really love someone,
They'll want you just for you.
All that they'd be asking for
Is something we all need –
That's love and understanding,
As I hope you'll all agree.

Learn from your Child

I'm very proud of the children
Who take their dogs out for a wee;
They always pick up after them,
Which is really lovely to see.

It's a shame some adults
Don't follow their lead,
To keep the footpaths clean.
I wish they would open their eyes
And really start to see
The danger that's on the floor,
Which they just leave.

The droppings from a dog
Can cause diseases,
Which can affect your child's
Eyesight, so please
Try to be aware
Of what harm it can do,
Coz you wouldn't want your child
Hurt now, would you?

I hope you understand
The message I'm trying to get through,
To pick up your animals' mess
While walking them, too.
It only takes a second to pick up the mess,
So try to be clean and all will be
impressed.

Losing Someone

When you lose someone you love,
Whether it is family or a loved one,
It's really hard to accept it has happened,
Because deep down you just want them back.

Don't despair, they've gone somewhere nice,
Up into heaven where the stars shine so
bright,
They'll be watching over you all day and all
night,
Coz they'll want to look after you with all
their might.

It's never nice to lose someone close to you,
But if you can talk about it, it really does
help –
Remembering all the good times that you
shared together,
Remembering you will love them for ever
and ever.

So try and be brave at this very sad time,
They'd want you to carry on with living
your life,
They wouldn't want you to be unhappy for
very long,
So try to pick yourself up and try to be
strong.

Biking to Work

You'll always find me biking to work,
Whistling or singing some songs.
It's really beautiful in the mornings,
Seeing the animals in the field, running along.

Music is the first thing on my mind,
When I wake up early in the morning.
It motivates me to get on my bike,
To go to work without any moaning.

I love to go to work coz I live on my own,
It gives me company instead of being alone;
When you're working it never shows,
How lonely life can be, living on your own.

So I'm happy that I'm well enough to work,
Keeping busy and making lots of friends;
It's only at night-time I'm on my own,
So I can relax, then enjoy my bath in content.

Happy Christmas

As the warm, cosy log fire
Is burning so bright,
We look out of the window
And it's so lovely and white –
It really feels like Christmas.

In the cold of the night
We all must sleep soundly,
Keeping ever so quiet,
So Santa will leave everyone a present,
That will lie under the sparkling tree.
Then he'll disappear, never to be seen,
But we'll all know in our hearts,
That he has surely been.

As we all wake up on that special morning,
We all have a stretch with lots of yawning,
We leap out of bed and run down the stairs,
Opening presents with excitement as the
paper we tear.

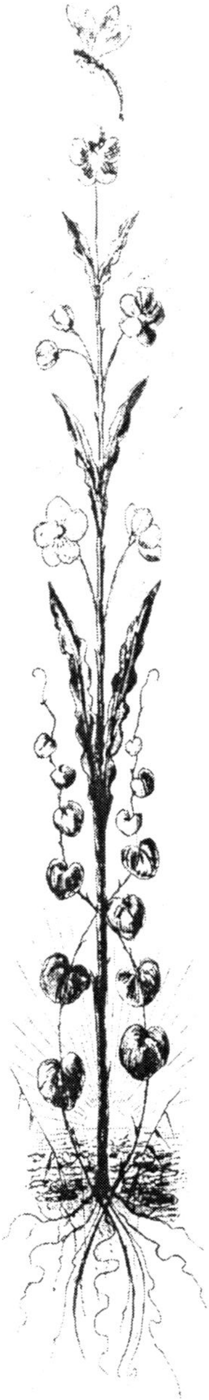

We Talked it Out

Sitting here all alone, I think to myself,
I'm really glad we could talk it through.
Speaking our minds and sorting things out
Was very sensible and the wisest thing to do.

Telling each other how we felt,
Then saying 'I love you',
Knowing it wouldn't have worked out,
Realising what we already knew.

Letting our emotions out
As we cuddled each other too.
Drying our eyes,
With tissues all over the room.

Both giving a sigh of relief
That we'd sorted it out so soon –
Now we can both be friends,
With our hearts knowing the truth.

At the Park

As I go for my daily walk in the park,
I see a nice young man in the distance,
I take a quick look, then look away,
Not wanting to scare him, wanting him to stay.

I find myself a bench to have a sit down,
Looking up very briefly as I'm reading my book,
Thinking to myself, *I wonder if he sees me*?
Then catching his eye, knowing that he's looked.

He comes over very slowly and asks to sit down,
I smile very sweetly, feeling nervous but very proud,
We start chatting and laughing both of us together,
We get on really well, like we have known each other for ever.

As we sit and chat, he turns and says,
'Would you like to go out for a meal one day?'
My answer was, 'Yes, that would be really great,'
So we think of somewhere nice for a date.

Leaving Me For Ever

It was nice while it lasted,
But now it has to end,
Oh I wish I could turn the clock back
And start all over again.
Knowing it could never be,
Hoping we can still be friends,
Coz my love for you will never die,
It'll be here till the very end.

Everywhere I go, I'm still thinking of you,
Feeling so confused, not knowing what to do.
Wondering what you're doing
As I live each year through,
Hoping you're thinking of me
As much as I think of you.

Knowing I'm on my own
As the days go by,
I'll treasure all the memories,
Which are floating in the sky.
Knowing that you loved me,
Even though you said goodbye,
Will keep my heart together,
When I miss you by my side.

To a Special Father

I'm glad you brought me into the world,
You really are so special to me,
I'm really lucky to be here at all,
I'm glad you're my father, for all to see.

From a very young age
You taught me all I know,
Even though I got into mischief,
You never let anger show.
You never stopped advising me
On how life should be;
I'm glad you were there to guide me,
This I could always see.

You were caring and kind
And always thoughtful to me,
You were there when I was in need,
When I was low and feeling down.
You always cheered me up,
And knew how to lift my frown.

People's Thoughts

The way the world goes round
Is such a sight to see,
For all the people in it
Will never understand me.

People can be hurtful,
Others can be nice,
Some are very friendly,
Others can bring fright.

We all think we're so lonely,
But it's just in our heads,
Coz all the people around us
Would help us if they could.

People can be cheerful,
Although you'd never know,
They just don't show their feelings
But inside their hearts glow.

Special Sister

You're such a special sister to me,
You're kind, caring and lovely to see,
I really hope that you do believe
How much you really mean to me.

Knowing you're doing well,
Living life as it should be,
Happy with your family,
Gives me more joy than I can tell.

With your amazing sense of humour,
You're fabulous to be around,
You make people really happy,
Instead of them having a frown.

Broken Glass

It's really such a shame
That some people have no respect,
Leaving broken bottles all over the floor,
Do they know the people they affect?

As you walk round the paths
After a Friday and Saturday night,
The amount of shattered glass you tread on,
You'd think they'd done it for spite.

Some people have walking difficulties,
Which this terrible mess doesn't help,
And if they should fall over one day,
They could end up hurting themselves.

People should also think of the dogs –
When owners take dogs for a walk,
They might not see the danger
Coz they are chatting and having a talk.
If they are not fully alert,
The dog could end up getting cut or hurt.

So please think twice
Before dropping things on the ground;
Put your rubbish in the bin
So humans and dogs can walk around.

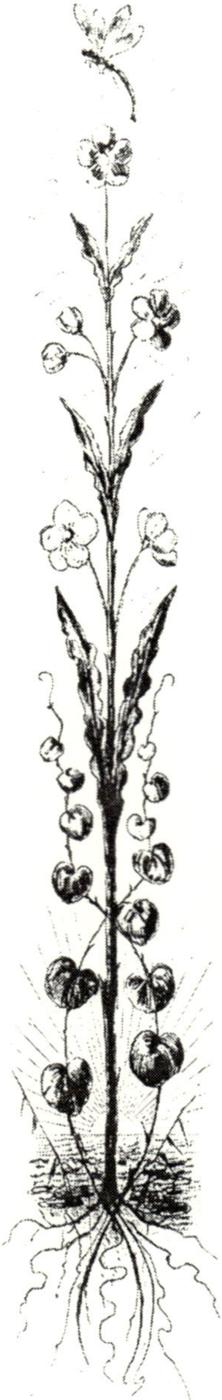

Sorry You're Leaving

I'm so sorry you are leaving,
The place won't be the same without you there,
You're always bringing a smile to my face,
With the laughter and cheekiness you share.

I've observed you've always worked hard,
All your workmates think you're great!
We will all miss you when you go through that door,
So we hope you'll come back and visit some more.

You're a special young lady, it's true to say,
As long as you're happy, things are certain to go your way.
So keep that smile on your face every day,
And be happy with your life for the rest of your days.

Let the Children Be Heard

We should listen and learn from our children,
Give them a chance to say what's on their minds,
They see the world so very differently,
Not hiding how they feel deep inside.

They never question how they're feeling,
They always tell the truth, not knowing how to lie,
Each individual has different ideas,
They are all so innocent and some very shy.

Some are so pleasant and can also be kind,
Some are naughty with mischief racing through their minds;
No child is exactly the same, that you will come to realise,
Even when you really get to know them, they'll still be able to surprise!

Children are so different, just like the stars in the sky,
They all have their own personalities, which comes as no surprise;
So try to understand them and surely you will find
They have so much to give when you look deep into their minds.

Constant Liar

If you're a constant liar,
It's a shameful thing to be –
Once people find out,
You really need to plead.

You need to show
You are remorseful
To the people,
You've hurt the most,
Especially to the friends
Who have been there for you.
Otherwise you'll lose them,
And then what will you do?

It's not very nice
To go alone through life.
If you don't try to correct
What you have done,
You'll regret it
For the rest of your life.
Be honest and true,
And good fortune will follow you.

Best Friend

A good friend
Is very hard to find,
So when you find
That special person,
Respect them and be good to them
All the while,
Let them know you're always
There for them with a smile.

Even if things go wrong,
You'll be there through thick and thin,
To protect them and be strong,
To keep them smiling and carry on.
You know you've got that bond,
You'll be together for however long.

Let them know
You appreciate their kindness
Even if you end up,
Having your ups and downs –
You'll never agree on everything,
So you might end up having a few rows.

They know at the back of their mind,
You'll do anything for them at any time,
So try not to be judgemental or hasty
And say something bad
That's playing on your mind.
You'll only regret it
If you say something nasty,
So always remember to be kind.

Be my Valentine

I hope that you will accept
This special offer I'm making today
To take you out on the town –
For dinner without further delay.
A romantic candle-lit meal
So I can tell you how I feel.

Your eyes, they sparkle
Like the stars in the sky;
Your smile always,
Leaves me on a high;
My heart misses a beat
When I see you down the street.

I need to know,
One way or the other,
If you are interested,
Or do you have another?
No worries if
You're otherwise engaged;
I will just start again,
And open a new page.

Whitchurch

Whitchurch is an historical place,
You can go to the local café
And have a cup of tea,
The buildings are very old,
Most of them black and white,
So it's really great to study
And then explore all the sights.

Most people are very pleasant
To whomever walks by,
They will greet you with a smile
Even if they feel shy.
There are plenty of churches,
To look at and visit,
There are also the gardens,
Where you can reminisce.

After doing your shopping,
If you fancy a rest,
Just pop into Walker's café,
You can have a chat and be their guest.
Everybody is so friendly,
You can always have a laugh,
So just take a chance and visit,
And I'm sure you'll love the staff.

Sixteen

You're sixteen and as sweet as can be,
Doing your utmost to be good,
Which I am very proud to see.
You've worked hard on your exams,
And now you're at college doing well too,
I know you'll do well, coz I see it in you.

I know you'll succeed at your goals in life,
You've got the stamina and also the fight,
Your friends and family will be so proud
of you,
They'll shout you a night out on the town.

So enjoy your life, right up until the end,
You're only here once, so never be afraid.
Look after yourself and never pretend
Or hide how you feel, especially with your
friends.

Moving On

Congratulations on getting your job,
I knew you'd do well,
As you're a lovely girl, who's nice to all;
You will go far, I can feel it, stand tall.

We wish you well on your journey ahead,
You'll always be in our hearts and in our heads,
You will not be forgotten as you walk through the door,
Just make sure you visit, we won't ask for more.

We hope your job is a big hit with you,
We hope you enjoy it through and through,
Lots of friends you are sure to make,
Coz you're nice to all and you're so great.

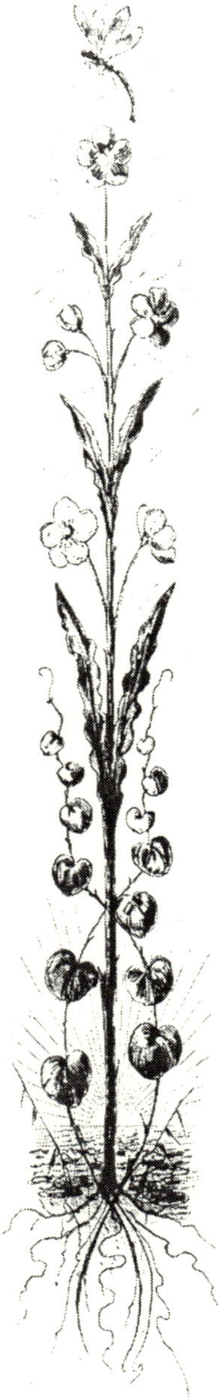

Hurting Inside

You know how ladies feel about you,
But still you don't care, it's true;
You think too much of yourself –
To think about others would confuse you.

Your self-obsession,
You never question.
You always come first
Or you make such a fuss;
Having your own way
Is always a must.
Otherwise you get in a temper.
Make complaints, then just
Sulk for hours.
Until you have your own way.
You're just like a child
Who's told he can't play.

You've got to grow up
And become a man.
Treat ladies with more respect
And then take a stand.
Take them for a walk,
Holding their hand,
Let them know you'll change
From a boy to a man,
Not wanting everything
To always go your way.
Be willing to work things out
And promise that you'll stay.

It's No Good Pretending

This pretence I keep up each day
About you and me, is a lie.
I do not want to cry
And so I find another way.

I'm scared of being alone,
No matter how hard I try,
But being together so long
Has made me realise,
I'm just going to have to leave
And make it on my own.

Even though we do agree
Our love was really strong,
It will all be better for me
Once I can move on.

In My Dreams

Night by night I dream of you,
Of being close and by your side.
If this should ever come to be,
I'd be so happy, deep inside.

I know you'll be there one day
And I'm prepared to sit and wait,
For I know you'll be so special,
It won't matter how long it takes.

I see you in the distance,
I can hardly believe my eyes,
You're just what I imagined,
And now you're in my life.

You know I'll never leave you,
I hope you feel the same way too,
It took a while to find you, my love,
Losing you, I'd never do.

Rest Your Body

You keep on rolling,
You keep on strolling,
Until your body gives up.
You sleep from midnight,
Get up at daybreak,
Knowing you'll never give up.

Your body feels weary,
Your legs go dreary,
Yet your brain tells you to do some more;
You feel like dropping,
But there's no stopping,
While your feet are touching the floor.

You work all hours,
To make some money,
But what is it all in aid of?
When the weekend comes,
You want to have fun,
But you know there's no end to it all.

You need to settle and take some rest,
Or you won't be here much longer.
Just take my warning,
Or else I'll be mourning
That you never took time to get stronger.
So don't be hasty, take a seat,
Try to relax and put up your feet.

Trail Bike

At the tender age of sixteen,
I went and bought a trail bike.
It was an amazing new experience,
Which I can honestly say I liked.

I could afford to buy it myself,
Because I had a good job.
I saved from the age of thirteen,
So I was happy, instead of being a slob.

I would go up to the empty field,
Put posts up in a straight line,
Then weave in and out of them,
While the weather was fine.

I wasn't allowed on the main road,
Because my father worried so,
But all the fields and back roads,
Were such boring places to go.

So I decided to go for my driving test,
It took a while to get used to the car,
But after a few lessons I was ready,
And passed – and celebrated in a bar!

Living Abroad

I couldn't have predicted
I'd finally get this chance,
It really is a dream come true,
It makes me want to dance.

My stomachs full of butterflies,
My pulse is racing fast,
I'm certain I can make it work,
I'm off abroad at last.

I know I'll be really nervous,
Living in a strange land,
But it's what I've always wanted to do,
I hope you understand.
Being independent is all that I am,
I know I'm going to like it,
I know it won't be a sham.

I will miss all my friends,
That I've made over the years,
But they will all be in my heart,
My thoughts, and sometimes my tears.
So I hope you will all wish me well,
On my journey with some cheers;
I will be in touch very soon,
To celebrate with some beers.

Young at Heart

When I was just a little girl,
I loved to run and hide and play,
Up past the bright and windy wood,
Then back down through the garden gate.

Being young is so very nice,
Being old can ruin your sight,
So make the most of everything,
Enjoy yourself with all your might.

I loved to climb the trees,
Way up so high,
I loved to feel the breeze,
And watch the clear blue sky.

I'd break the branches off,
Then find a length of string,
To make myself a bow and arrow,
I'd then play till the spring.

I miss being a little girl,
When all I did was play,
Coz when you reach a certain age
You have to earn your pay;
You have to find a job
To get you through the day,
Coz nobody does nothing for nothing,
Unless things are going their way.

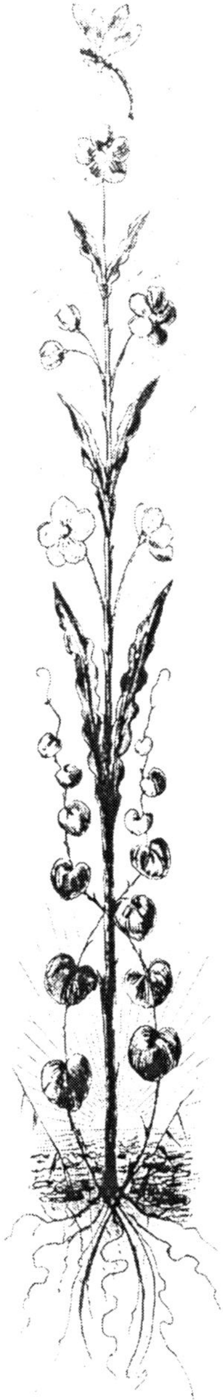

We Made It

We walked side by side
Along the sandy beach –
His hand touching mine,
Then holding,
Our eyes then would meet.

My eyes they feel so starry,
I am happy with all my heart,
I've never been so cheerful,
So don't ever make it stop.

I'm so glad I found my man,
I really love him with all my heart,
I know this feeling will never leave,
I just know I can't be wrong.

The sea's so lovely and blue,
With the sun shining through,
It feels so very romantic,
With us being here too.

Printed in the United Kingdom
by Lightning Source UK Ltd.
129050UK00001B/130/P

9 781847 482679